HACKERS EXPOSED: 143 REVEALING INSIGHTS AND QUIZ GAME

Satoshi street

www.satoshi-street.com

Visited for more

1

Table of Contents

5

ABOUT THE AUTHOR

Satoshi Street is a mysterious figure in the realms of finance, technology, and ethical hacking, and also a published author and crypto enthusiast. With unwavering belief in the future of cryptocurrency and its potential for financial gain, Satoshi has become a prominent figure in the crypto community.

Satoshi's journey began when they first discovered Bitcoin, sparking an immediate fascination with the world of cryptocurrency. This fascination led to a deep dive into the study and trading of cryptocurrencies, driven by the vision of a decentralized, borderless financial system. Over time, Satoshi's expertise in the cryptocurrency space grew, and they became a sought-after authority in the field.

However, Satoshi offers more than just financial expertise. They are also a gifted writer, known for their ability to simplify complex financial concepts and present them in an engaging and accessible manner. Many individuals have had their first introduction to the intriguing realm of crypto through Satoshi's writings.

In addition to their extensive knowledge of cryptocurrencies, Satoshi has penned a new book that shares their wisdom and experience with the world. This book offers a wealth of strategies for profiting from cryptocurrencies and delves into topics such as understanding various coins and tokens and optimizing your engagement with the cryptocurrency market. Satoshi's writing style is not only informative but also entertaining, making it an invaluable resource for those looking to learn more about cryptography or to step into the field.

Satoshi Street's boundless enthusiasm and expertise in ethical hacking and cryptocurrency are sure to inspire and educate both seasoned traders and curious newcomers. If you are interested in the world of cryptocurrency trading and investment or wish to explore the ethical aspects of hacking, follow Satoshi's lead and discover the exciting opportunities this realm has to offer.

AUTHOR NAME

Satoshi street

FOREWORD

In the fast-evolving world of technology and cybersecurity, knowledge is power, and understanding the tools and techniques employed by both white hat and black hat hackers is paramount. "Hackers Exposed: 143 Revealing Insights" is a comprehensive journey into the realm of hacking, bringing to light the hidden intricacies of the digital world. This book is not just a mere collection of facts; it is a profound exploration of the ever-expanding landscape of hacking, featuring captivating stories, insights, and practical knowledge.

Why This Book Is Incredibly Engaging

"Hackers Exposed: 143 Revealing Insights" stands out as an exceptional resource for several reasons:

143 Fascinating Facts: We've meticulously curated a vast array of facts that span the entire spectrum of hacking. From the early exploits of pioneering hackers to the latest trends in cybersecurity, these 143 facts offer a captivating and in-depth look at the world of hacking.

Unveiling the Shadows: Our journey begins with the shadowy history of hacking, delving into the origins of computer worms, the birth of computer viruses, and the legendary tales of notorious

hackers like Kevin Mitnick. Each story is a testament to the transformative power of curiosity and ingenuity in the digital age.

Understanding the Motivations: We explore the intricate motivations behind hacking, from the ethical hackers who protect systems to hacktivists fighting for a better world, and the murky world of state-sponsored cyber weapons exemplified by the Stuxnet worm. These insights shed light on the diverse motivations that drive hackers.

Revealing Cybersecurity's Secrets: Chapter 5 takes you into the intricate world of cybersecurity, showcasing the invisible defenders, the ongoing arms race, and the ever-present human element in cyber resilience. Discover the ethical dilemmas, the role of governments, and the looming quantum threat.

A Glimpse into Hacking Tools and Techniques: Chapter 7 is an in-depth exploration of hacking tools, offering insights into penetration testing tools, password cracking tools, vulnerability scanners, and more. These tools are the building blocks of both defenders and attackers, and understanding them is key to staying ahead in the cybersecurity game.

Practical Code Examples and Tools List: To enhance your understanding and provide a hands-on experience, we've included practical code examples and a comprehensive list of hacking tools. Whether you're a cybersecurity enthusiast, a professional, or just curious, these resources will help you navigate the world of hacking effectively.

"Hackers Exposed: 143 Revealing Insights" is not just a book; it's an immersive journey that demystifies the world of hacking.

Whether you're seeking knowledge for professional growth, cybersecurity defense, or simply to satisfy your curiosity, this book is your guide to the captivating and dynamic world of hacking. Join us as we uncover the secrets, stories, and strategies of hackers, both ethical and malicious, in this ever-evolving digital landscape.

CHAPTER 01

THE WORLD OF HACKERS

In the enigmatic realm where bits and bytes hold the keys to power, hackers are the modern-day explorers. These digital adventurers, often hidden in the shadows, have shaped our interconnected world in ways both beneficial and treacherous. Let's embark on a journey to uncover the mystique of hackers and their profound impact on technology and society.

Fact 1: In the cryptic origins of hacking, the term "hacker" did not connote mischief but rather celebrated the brilliance of clever programmers. They were the visionaries who crafted innovative solutions to perplexing tech problems. The evolution of this word mirrors the shifting landscape of hacking itself.

Fact 2: When computers were in their infancy, hackers emerged as pioneers. They laid the foundation for the modern tech landscape, exploring uncharted territory and shaping the digital world that we now navigate.

Fact 3: The annals of hacking history bear witness to a notorious moment—the birth of the Morris Worm in 1988. This cunning piece of code disrupted the nascent internet and served as a harbinger of a new era of cybersecurity challenges.

Fact 4: Hacking's roots trace back to the early '70s, where the world witnessed the emergence of the very first computer virus, "Creeper." Created as an experiment, this proto-malware set the stage for the malware we battle today.

Fact 5: One name stands out in the annals of hacking: Kevin Mitnick. Dubbed the world's most famous hacker, Mitnick utilized social engineering skills to infiltrate highly secure systems, weaving a tale of intrigue and danger.

Fact 6: The ethical side of hacking, often referred to as "white hat" hacking, is a noble endeavor. Organizations employ these cybersecurity experts to unearth vulnerabilities before malicious hackers can exploit them. It's a continuous battle between good and evil in the digital realm.

Fact 7: Some hackers are motivated by ideology, championing hacktivism—a form of digital protest. The hacktivist group Anonymous is one example, unveiling government secrets and corporate injustices to the world.

Fact 8: The world of hacking witnessed a significant shift with Stuxnet, a highly sophisticated worm believed to be the first state-

sponsored cyberweapon. Designed to target Iran's nuclear facilities, it underscored the political ramifications of hacking.

Fact 9: On the darker side, black hat hackers navigate the digital underworld for personal gain. They engage in activities such as stealing sensitive data, launching cyberattacks for profit, or conducting acts of digital espionage.

Fact 10: Hacking isn't confined to the virtual realm. Malicious hackers have extended their reach, manipulating everything from traffic lights to medical devices, posing profound risks to public safety and security.

Fact 11: The ominous "Zero-Day Exploit" looms large in the hacking world. It refers to vulnerabilities in software unknown to the software vendor—a prime target for hackers looking to exploit weaknesses in systems.

Fact 12: A name etched in the history of whistleblowing and digital exposure is Julian Assange, the founder of WikiLeaks. His actions revealed classified information from around the globe, shaking the foundations of conventional secrecy.

This is just the beginning of our journey into the intriguing world of hacking, where technology, innovation, and subversion converge. As we delve deeper into this domain, we'll unravel more mysteries and unveil the secrets that have shaped our digital landscape.

CHAPTER 02

THE DARK SIDE OF HACKING HISTORY

As we embark on this journey into the depths of hacking history, we find ourselves immersed in a world where ingenuity, cunning, and sometimes outright chaos reign. In this chapter, we delve into the enigmatic stories that define the darkest moments in the annals of hacking, featuring the Morris Worm, the inception of the computer virus "Creeper," and the legendary tale of Kevin Mitnick.

2.1 The Morris Worm: The First Known Computer Worm

Fact 1: In the tumultuous year of 1988, the digital realm was shaken to its core by the emergence of the notorious Morris Worm. Crafted by a young and enterprising computer science student named Robert Tappan Morris, this self-replicating code was meant to be a harmless experiment. Yet, it spiraled wildly out of control, inadvertently infecting thousands of computers across the nascent internet, far beyond Morris's initial intentions.

Fact 2: The Morris Worm's genesis lay in Morris's insatiable curiosity, leading him to concoct this experiment aimed at gauging the internet's size. Alas, an innocent programming error proved catastrophic as it unleashed a wave of rampant replication, causing widespread disruption. This unintended consequence sent shockwaves throughout the digital realm, underscoring the pressing need for robust cybersecurity measures and responsible hacking practices.

Fact 3: The chaos sown by the Morris Worm was a pivotal moment in the history of the internet, prompting the establishment of the Computer Emergency Response Team (CERT). This organization emerged as a bulwark against future network security incidents, galvanizing efforts to enhance cybersecurity awareness across the burgeoning digital landscape.

2.2 The Birth of the Computer Virus "Creeper"

Fact 4: Journeying back to the early 1970s, the dawn of the computer age saw the birth of the very first computer virus known as "Creeper." Conceived as part of an experiment by engineer Bob

Thomas at BBN Technologies, this virus served a unique purpose—testing the vulnerabilities of the ARPANET, the precursor to the modern internet.

Fact 5: In stark contrast to the malevolent viruses of today, Creeper exhibited a relatively benign behavior. It would manifest as a message on infected computers, bearing the playful challenge, "I'm the creeper, catch me if you can!" This digital game of tag saw the virus merrily leap from one system to another, creating a phenomenon akin to a whimsical chase.

Fact 6: The presence of Creeper heralded the dawn of antivirus solutions. "Reaper," the world's first antivirus program, was conceived as a direct response to the benign Creeper virus. Reaper's primary mission was to locate and eradicate the Creeper virus from infected computers, marking a significant milestone in the evolution of cybersecurity.

2.3 The Legendary Saga of Kevin Mitnick

Fact 7: Kevin Mitnick, renowned as the world's most famous hacker, wielded a unique talent—social engineering. His exploits were marked by ingenious manipulation of individuals rather than direct digital intrusion. Notable among his feats was gaining unauthorized access to Pacific Bell's voicemail computers, a feat achieved through clever ruses.

Fact 8: Mitnick's mastery of social engineering was nothing short of legendary. Frequently, he would assume the identities of trusted figures to extract confidential information. In one audacious instance, he posed as a Pacific Bell technician, artfully persuading employees to grant him access to their systems.

Fact 9: The pursuit of Mitnick by law enforcement agencies unfolded as a captivating cat-and-mouse game. His evasion tactics included the use of cloned cellular phones and the fabrication of false identities, rendering his capture a monumental challenge.

Fact 10: Remarkably, Mitnick's eventual arrest and imprisonment did not extinguish his passion for hacking. After serving his sentence, he metamorphosed into a respected security consultant and author, leveraging his profound understanding of hacking to aid organizations in fortifying their defenses.

These narratives unveil the intriguing, sometimes perilous facets of hacking history, where curiosity, experimentation, and the relentless pursuit of knowledge could give rise to far-reaching and often unintended consequences in the ever-evolving digital realm.

CHAPTER 03

TYPES AND MOTIVATIONS OF HACKING

In the ever-evolving world of hacking, motivations range from the noble to the nefarious. This chapter unveils the multifaceted nature of hacking, featuring the ethical hackers, the hacktivists striving for a better world, and the shadowy world of state-sponsored cyber weapons exemplified by the enigmatic Stuxnet.

3.1 Ethical Hacking: The Good Guys in Cyberspace

Fact 1: Ethical hacking, often referred to as "white hat" hacking, embodies a digital heroism that safeguards the virtual realm. These cybersecurity experts are not foes but allies, employed by organizations to uncover vulnerabilities before malicious hackers can exploit them. They are the vigilant guardians of digital integrity.

Fact 2: Ethical hackers don't break the law; they follow a strict code of ethics. Their mission includes conducting penetration tests, identifying security weaknesses, and proposing remedies. In essence, they act as a digital first line of defense, preventing breaches before they occur.

Fact 3: The line between ethical hackers and malicious hackers can blur, leading to the intriguing concept of "gray hat" hackers. These individuals, motivated by the pursuit of knowledge and security, occasionally tread the thin line between right and wrong.

Fact 4: Ethical hackers often engage in "bug bounty" programs, where companies reward them for discovering and responsibly disclosing security vulnerabilities. This practice helps organizations improve their cybersecurity posture.

Fact 5: The realm of ethical hacking demands continuous learning and adaptation. As the hacking landscape evolves, ethical hackers must stay updated with the latest threats and countermeasures.

3.2 Hacktivism: Hacking for a Better World

Fact 6: Hacktivism represents the fusion of hacking and activism, where digital tools are harnessed to bring about societal or political change. Groups like Anonymous are emblematic of this movement, using their skills to expose government secrets and corporate injustices in the name of justice.

Fact 7: Notable hacktivist actions have included distributed denial of service (DDoS) attacks, website defacements, and data leaks. These tactics serve as digital protests aimed at highlighting issues and advocating for transparency.

Fact 8: While hacktivism often garners attention for its headline-grabbing actions, it's a controversial space with a spectrum of motivations. Some view hacktivists as modern heroes, while others see them as digital vigilantes.

Fact 9: Hacktivists are driven by a sense of moral duty and may use their skills to support causes ranging from free speech and online privacy to political transparency and social justice.

Fact 10: The line between hacktivism and cybercrime can be blurry, leading to legal and ethical debates about the impact and legitimacy of hacktivist actions.

3.3 State-Sponsored Cyber Weapons and Stuxnet

Fact 11: The world of state-sponsored cyber weapons has ushered in a new era of geopolitical intrigue. One of the most notorious examples is Stuxnet, a highly sophisticated worm believed to be the first state-sponsored cyberweapon. It was designed to target Iran's nuclear facilities, underscoring the political and destructive capabilities of hacking.

Fact 12: Stuxnet's development involved an array of advanced techniques, including exploiting zero-day vulnerabilities, subverting digital certificates, and evading detection. Its creators

*demonstrated the potential for nation-states to wield cyber
weapons as tools of political influence and warfare.*

*Fact 13: Stuxnet is not an isolated case. Many nations have
invested heavily in offensive cyber capabilities, resulting in a
cyber arms race that parallels traditional arms races. This silent
battleground is reshaping the dynamics of global security and
espionage.*

*The world of hacking unfolds as a multifaceted tapestry of
motivations, from the ethical sentinels safeguarding the digital
realm to hacktivists striving for change and state-sponsored cyber
weapons wielding power in the shadows. In this intricate
landscape, hacking is a tool of both creation and destruction, a
reflection of the ever-changing face of our interconnected world.*

THE WORLD OF BLACK HATS

Welcome to a realm where shadows conceal nefarious intentions and tools of malevolence are wielded with malicious purpose. Within this chapter, we'll delve deeper into the enigmatic world of black hat hackers, exploring their treacherous motives, and the shadowy tools they employ.

4.1 Black Hat Hacker: The Dark Artisans of Cyberspace

Fact 1: Black hat hackers, the dark sorcerers of the digital domain, wield their skills with malevolence in mind. They infiltrate systems, pilfer sensitive data, and undermine digital security. Their motives span a spectrum from cybercrime to espionage, casting a chilling aura over the digital landscape.

Fact 2: Avarice fuels the ambitions of black hat hackers, often leading them down the treacherous path of financial gain. Their arsenal includes a repertoire of sinister activities like identity theft, credit card fraud, and ruthless ransomware attacks designed to extort ill-gotten wealth from their victims.

Fact 3: The cloak of anonymity shrouds black hat hackers as they employ an arsenal of tools. Among these, Remote Access Trojans (RATs) serve as potent instruments, enabling covert entry into victims' computers. These insidious pests bestow malefactors control over systems, granting access to a trove of sensitive data.

Fact 4: Keyloggers, a noxious form of malware, find frequent application in the dark arts of black hat hackers. These digital snares surreptitiously capture keystrokes, ensnaring login credentials and pilfering personal information, weaving a web of deceit.

4.2 Hacks in the Physical World: From Traffic Lights to Medical Devices

Fact 5: The insidious reach of hacking transcends the boundaries of the digital realm, encroaching upon the tangible world. Incidents include the malevolent manipulation of traffic lights, compromising critical infrastructure, and even infiltrating the sanctity of medical devices like insulin pumps.

Fact 6: A chilling reality emerges as researchers unveil vulnerabilities in medical devices such as pacemakers and insulin pumps. These revelations send shivers down the spines of society, illuminating the pressing need for fortified security in the age of the Internet of Things (IoT).

Fact 7: Tools such as the Internet of Things (IoT) Scanner become dark allies, enabling malevolent actors to identify and exploit the weaknesses of vulnerable IoT devices. This digital cartography maps a sinister journey through the interconnected tapestry of technology.

4.3 Zero-Day Exploits and Their Threat to the Cyber World

Fact 8: In the shadows, black hat hackers avidly seek zero-day exploits, hidden vulnerabilities concealed from the vigilant eyes of software vendors. These clandestine vulnerabilities serve as enigmatic keys for executing covert and effective digital assaults.

Fact 9: The malevolent and the vigilant alike turn to the beguiling embrace of exploit frameworks such as Metasploit. This compendium of treacherous tools offers an extensive arsenal for testing and breaching systems, encompassing both the malefactor and the digital sentry.

Fact 10: The dark web emerges as a thriving marketplace for the trade of zero-day exploits. Illicit bazaars beckon cybercriminals with the alluring prospect of purchasing exploits, casting shadows over unsuspecting victims who may bear the brunt of these sinister wares.

Within this chapter, we plunge deeper into the labyrinthine world of black hat hackers, where malevolent intentions manifest in a multitude of forms and the tools of darkness threaten both the digital and physical realms. The significance of cybersecurity becomes all the more pronounced in a world ever more interconnected and vulnerable to the machinations of these shadowy figures.

CHAPTER 05

THE INVISIBLE DEFENDERS: CYBERSECURITY

In the digital battleground where black hats and white hats wage their invisible wars, cybersecurity stands as the sentinel guarding our interconnected world. Within this chapter, we'll uncover the secrets of these invisible defenders, their relentless efforts, and the arsenal of tools they wield to protect us.

5.1 The Guardians of Cyberspace

Fact 1: Cybersecurity professionals, the silent guardians of the digital realm, stand watch over the complex labyrinth of the internet. Their mission is to safeguard data, protect systems, and mitigate threats posed by an ever-evolving landscape of cyber risks.

Fact 2: In their ceaseless quest to defend against cyber threats, cybersecurity experts employ a multifaceted approach, combining technology, policies, and human vigilance. This holistic strategy is crucial in the face of the evolving tactics of cybercriminals.

Fact 3: Encryption, a cornerstone of modern cybersecurity, cloaks sensitive data in an impenetrable shroud of secrecy. Without decryption keys, even the most sophisticated adversaries find themselves thwarted by the veil of cryptographic protection.

5.2 The Constant Arms Race

Fact 4: Cybersecurity is an unending arms race between defenders and attackers. As security measures evolve, so do the tactics of cybercriminals, necessitating constant adaptation and innovation by cybersecurity professionals.

Fact 5: Zero-day vulnerabilities, undiscovered by software vendors, represent the greatest vulnerabilities. Cybersecurity experts diligently hunt for these hidden chinks in the digital armor to patch them before malicious hackers exploit them.

Fact 6: Machine learning and artificial intelligence play pivotal roles in cybersecurity, enabling the identification of anomalies and patterns that escape human observation. These technologies empower defenders to stay one step ahead of cyber adversaries.

5.3 The Menace of Phishing Attacks

Fact 7: Phishing attacks are among the most common and insidious threats on the internet. Cybercriminals deploy cunning schemes to deceive individuals into revealing personal information, including usernames and passwords.

Fact 8: Spear-phishing is a more targeted form of phishing, tailored to exploit specific individuals or organizations. Attackers gather personal information to craft convincing messages, increasing their chances of success.

Fact 9: Cybersecurity experts utilize email filtering tools to detect and quarantine phishing emails, reducing the risk of employees falling victim to these deceptive schemes.

5.4 The Looming Shadow of Ransomware

Fact 10: Ransomware attacks have surged in recent years, causing widespread havoc. Cybercriminals employ malicious software to encrypt victims' data, demanding a ransom for its release. In many cases, victims are left with no choice but to pay.

Fact 11: The best defense against ransomware is a robust backup system. Regularly backing up critical data to offline or cloud storage can mitigate the impact of a ransomware attack.

5.5 The Challenge of IoT Security

Fact 12: The Internet of Things (IoT) has expanded the attack surface, as interconnected devices often lack robust security measures. Cybersecurity experts grapple with the task of securing a vast and diverse array of IoT devices.

Fact 13: Secure boot and firmware updates are essential to maintaining the security of IoT devices. Ensuring that only trusted firmware can be executed is critical to prevent unauthorized access.

5.6 The Ongoing Battle for Cyber Resilience

Fact 14: Cyber resilience is the ability to withstand, recover from, and adapt to cyberattacks. It's a fundamental aspect of modern cybersecurity, encompassing not only prevention but also response and recovery.

Fact 15: Cybersecurity experts conduct "red team" exercises, where ethical hackers simulate cyberattacks to test an organization's defenses. These simulations reveal vulnerabilities that need to be addressed.

Fact 16: The European Union's General Data Protection Regulation (GDPR) has established stringent requirements for data protection. Organizations worldwide must comply with these regulations when handling the personal data of EU citizens.

5.7 The Ethical Dilemmas of Cybersecurity

Fact 17: Ethical dilemmas often arise in cybersecurity. For example, when cybersecurity experts discover vulnerabilities, they must decide whether to disclose them to the public or report them to the affected organization.

Fact 18: The debate over "hacking back" is another ethical quandary. Some argue that retaliatory cyberattacks against cybercriminals are necessary, while others believe they could escalate conflicts and cause collateral damage.

5.8 The Future of Cybersecurity

Fact 19: The future of cybersecurity is closely tied to emerging technologies such as quantum computing, which could render current encryption methods obsolete. Preparing for the quantum threat is a significant challenge.

Fact 20: As society becomes increasingly reliant on technology, the need for skilled cybersecurity professionals is growing exponentially. Cybersecurity is a dynamic field with abundant career opportunities.

5.9 The Human Element in Cybersecurity

Fact 21: People play a crucial role in cybersecurity. Training and awareness programs are essential to educate individuals about the risks of cyber threats and promote safe online practices.

Fact 22: Social engineering, where attackers manipulate individuals to reveal sensitive information, remains a potent threat. Human vigilance is often the last line of defense against such attacks.

Fact 23: The concept of "security by design" is gaining traction, with organizations integrating security into the development process from the outset rather than as an afterthought.

5.10 The Enigmatic Dark Web

Fact 24: The dark web serves as a clandestine marketplace for cybercriminals, offering a wide range of illicit goods and services, from stolen data to hacking tools.

Fact 25: Cybersecurity experts often monitor the dark web for signs of impending cyberattacks and to discover if their organization's data is being traded or sold.

Fact 26: The dark web's anonymity and encryption make it a haven for illegal activities, making it challenging for law enforcement to track and apprehend cybercriminals.

5.11 The Vital Role of Government in Cybersecurity

Fact 27: Governments worldwide have established agencies and regulations to combat cyber threats. These agencies work to protect critical infrastructure and respond to cyber incidents.

Fact 28: International collaboration is essential in the fight against cybercrime. Cybersecurity is a global challenge that

CHAPTER 06

THE FUTURE OF HACKING

In this chapter, we venture into the uncharted territory of the future of hacking. As technology advances at an unprecedented pace, so too do the opportunities and challenges for hackers. Explore the cutting-edge developments, emerging trends, and the potential impacts that lie ahead.

6.1 The Rise of AI-Powered Hacking

Fact 1: Artificial intelligence (AI) has become a double-edged sword in the realm of hacking. While AI-driven cybersecurity tools are improving defenses, malicious hackers are also leveraging AI to conduct more sophisticated attacks.

Fact 2: AI-powered malware can autonomously adapt and evolve to evade detection, making it a formidable adversary for cybersecurity professionals. These intelligent programs can identify vulnerabilities, devise attack strategies, and launch assaults with alarming precision.

Fact 3: AI is being harnessed to automate and streamline social engineering attacks. Chatbots and deepfake technologies enable hackers to engage with targets, making it increasingly challenging to discern the real from the virtual.

6.2 Quantum Computing and Cryptography

Fact 4: The emergence of quantum computing threatens current encryption methods. Quantum computers could break existing encryption algorithms, rendering data vulnerable to interception.

Fact 5: Post-quantum cryptography is a burgeoning field, with researchers developing encryption techniques that can withstand quantum attacks. The future of cybersecurity hinges on these innovations.

Fact 6: The quantum internet, still in its infancy, promises ultra-secure communication using quantum key distribution. This technology could revolutionize data privacy.

6.3 IoT and the Expanding Attack Surface

Fact 7: The Internet of Things (IoT) continues to proliferate, introducing a vast array of interconnected devices into homes, businesses, and critical infrastructure. However, many IoT devices lack robust security features.

Fact 8: The expanding attack surface provided by IoT devices presents a significant challenge to cybersecurity. Vulnerabilities in these devices can be exploited to gain access to larger networks.

Fact 9: IoT security standards and regulations are being developed to mitigate risks and enhance the security of connected devices. However, compliance and enforcement remain complex issues.

6.4 Ransomware's Evolution

Fact 10: Ransomware attacks are evolving, with hackers demanding larger ransoms and targeting high-profile victims, including governments and large corporations.

Fact 11: The use of double extortion tactics has become common in ransomware attacks. In addition to encrypting data, hackers threaten to release sensitive information unless a ransom is paid.

Fact 12: Cyber insurance is on the rise as organizations seek protection against the financial fallout of ransomware attacks. However, the surge in claims is leading to increased premiums and stricter underwriting.

6.5 5G and Its Impact on Security

Fact 13: The rollout of 5G networks brings both promise and challenges for cybersecurity. While 5G offers faster and more reliable connectivity, it also introduces new vulnerabilities.

Fact 14: The increased volume of data transmitted through 5G networks presents opportunities for hackers to intercept and exploit this data. Security measures must evolve to keep pace with the network's capabilities.

Fact 15: The growth of the Internet of Everything (IoE), driven by 5G, will connect billions of devices and sensors, amplifying the need for robust security protocols to protect against potential threats.

6.6 Hacktivism in the Digital Age

Fact 16: Hacktivism continues to be a powerful force in the digital age, with hacktivist groups using their skills to advance causes related to freedom of speech, social justice, and government transparency.

Fact 17: The symbiotic relationship between hacktivists and the media ensures that their actions receive widespread attention, influencing public discourse and pressuring organizations to address critical issues.

Fact 18: The boundaries of hacktivism blur as it evolves to include not only digital protests but also real-world actions, such as participating in political movements and exposing corporate misconduct.

6.7 The Ethical Hacking Renaissance

Fact 19: Ethical hacking is on the rise as organizations recognize the importance of proactive security testing. Certified Ethical Hackers (CEHs) are in high demand for their skills in identifying vulnerabilities before malicious hackers do.

Fact 20: Bug bounty programs have gained popularity, with companies offering financial rewards to ethical hackers who discover and responsibly disclose security vulnerabilities.

Fact 21: The community of ethical hackers is growing, and they often collaborate to address security issues collectively, leading to stronger digital defenses.

6.8 The Role of Cybersecurity Regulation

Fact 22: Governments worldwide are enacting cybersecurity regulations and data protection laws to safeguard their citizens' digital lives. Compliance with these laws is becoming essential for organizations.

Fact 23: The European Union's Cybersecurity Act, which establishes a framework for certifying the security of products and services, is a significant step toward enhancing digital security.

Fact 24: Data breach notification laws, such as the General Data Protection Regulation (GDPR) in the EU and the California Consumer Privacy Act (CCPA), compel organizations to promptly disclose breaches and provide affected individuals with information about the incident.

6.9 The Dark Web's Evolution

Fact 25: The dark web remains a shadowy underworld for cybercriminal activities, offering a wide range of illegal goods and services. Its evolution is characterized by increasing anonymity and a growing customer base.

Fact 26: Cryptocurrencies like Bitcoin continue to be the preferred method of payment on the dark web, enabling anonymous transactions that are difficult to trace.

Fact 27: Law enforcement agencies are working diligently to combat dark web marketplaces, leading to the takedown of several notorious sites and the arrest of their operators.

6.10 The Shifting Geopolitics of Cyber Warfare

Fact 28: Geopolitics plays a significant role in the world of cyber warfare. Nation-states are increasingly utilizing cyberattacks as tools of espionage, influence, and warfare.

Fact 29: The development and use of cyber weapons have the potential to alter the balance of power on the global stage, as cyberattacks can be carried out with a degree of secrecy and deniability.

Fact 30: International agreements and norms related to cyber warfare are still in their infancy, and establishing rules for cyber conflict remains a complex and evolving challenge.

6.11 The Human Element in Hacking

Fact 31: The human element remains a critical factor in the world of hacking. Social engineering, where attackers manipulate individuals to reveal sensitive information, continues to be a potent threat.

Fact 32: Awareness and education are essential in combating social engineering attacks. Regular training can help individuals recognize and resist manipulation attempts.

Fact 33: Insider threats, whether through malice or negligence, pose a significant challenge to cybersecurity. Organizations must implement robust monitoring and access controls to mitigate these risks.

6.12 Cybersecurity Workforce Shortage

Fact 34: The demand for cybersecurity professionals continues to outpace the supply. Organizations are struggling to fill key roles, and the shortage is expected to persist in the coming years.

Fact 35: The gender gap in the cybersecurity field is a pressing concern. Efforts are being made to promote diversity and encourage more women to pursue careers in cybersecurity.

Fact 36: The rise of remote work has introduced new security challenges, as organizations adapt to a more distributed workforce and the need for secure remote access solutions.

CHAPTER 07

THACKING TOOLS AND TECHNIQUES

In this chapter, we'll dive deep into the arsenal of hacking tools and techniques that have become essential in the world of cybersecurity. From penetration testing tools to malware creation, we'll explore the methods and software used by hackers and cybersecurity experts alike.

7.1 Penetration Testing Tools

Fact 1: Penetration testing, or ethical hacking, is a vital component of cybersecurity. It involves simulating cyberattacks to identify vulnerabilities in a system before malicious hackers exploit them.

Fact 2: One popular penetration testing tool is Metasploit, an open-source framework that aids security professionals in developing and executing exploits against target systems. It allows them to test the system's defenses.

Fact 3: Wireshark is a powerful network protocol analyzer used for capturing and examining data on a network. It helps identify potential vulnerabilities and security issues in network communications.

7.2 Password Cracking Tools

Fact 4: Passwords are a weak link in security. Password cracking tools, like John the Ripper and Hashcat, employ various techniques to decipher passwords, such as brute force attacks and dictionary attacks.

Fact 5: These tools can be used by both security professionals to test the strength of their own systems and malicious hackers to gain unauthorized access to accounts and data.

7.3 Vulnerability Scanners

Fact 6: Vulnerability scanners, such as Nessus and OpenVAS, automate the process of identifying and assessing vulnerabilities in systems and networks. They help organizations proactively address security weaknesses.

Fact 7: These tools often utilize a database of known vulnerabilities and employ various scanning techniques to discover potential weaknesses, including missing patches, misconfigurations, and open ports.

7.4 Web Application Testing Tools

Fact 8: Web applications are frequent targets for hackers. Tools like Burp Suite and OWASP ZAP are designed for web application security testing, identifying vulnerabilities like SQL injection, cross-site scripting (XSS), and more.

Fact 9: Automated tools are essential for efficiently scanning web applications for security issues, but manual testing and ethical hacking remain critical to uncovering complex vulnerabilities.

7.5 Malware Creation Tools

Fact 10: Unfortunately, hacking isn't limited to protecting systems. Malicious hackers create and deploy malware to compromise systems and steal data. Tools like RATs (Remote Access Trojans) and keyloggers are used in the development of malware.

Fact 11: The availability of malware creation kits, such as the infamous BlackHole Exploit Kit, has made it easier for even those with limited technical expertise to develop and distribute malware.

Fact 12: The rise of ransomware-as-a-service (RaaS) platforms allows cybercriminals to lease ransomware variants and share the ill-gotten profits with the developers.

7.6 Packet Sniffing Tools

Fact 13: Packet sniffing tools like tcpdump and Wireshark capture and analyze data packets transmitted over a network. These tools are crucial for network troubleshooting and security monitoring.

Fact 14: While these tools are essential for network professionals, they can also be misused by malicious hackers to eavesdrop on sensitive data, making encryption and secure communication essential.

7.7 Social Engineering Techniques

Fact 15: Social engineering is a powerful hacking technique that exploits human psychology to gain access to systems or information. Common tactics include phishing, pretexting, and tailgating.

Fact 16: Tools like GoPhish are used to conduct simulated phishing attacks as part of security awareness training. These tests help educate employees about the dangers of social engineering.

7.8 DDoS (Distributed Denial of Service) Tools

Fact 17: DDoS attacks flood a target's server or network with an overwhelming volume of traffic, causing service disruptions. Tools like LOIC (Low Orbit Ion Cannon) and Mirai have been used in high-profile DDoS attacks.

Fact 18: These tools have both legitimate uses, such as stress testing a network for resilience, and malicious purposes when wielded by hacktivists or cybercriminals.

7.9 Steganography Tools

Fact 19: Steganography is the practice of concealing information within other data, such as hiding a message within an image.

Tools like OpenStego and Steghide are used to embed and extract hidden data.

Fact 20: While steganography has legitimate uses in data protection, it can also be employed by hackers to covertly transmit malicious payloads or exfiltrate data.

7.10 Cryptography Tools

Fact 21: Cryptography tools are not only used for securing communications but can also be leveraged by hackers for encrypting malicious payloads or files. Common cryptography tools include GnuPG and OpenSSL.

Fact 22: Ethical hackers use these tools for legitimate purposes, such as verifying the integrity of software or ensuring the privacy of sensitive data.

7.11 Exploit Development Tools

Fact 23: Exploit development tools are essential for both ethical hackers and malicious attackers. Tools like Immunity Debugger and GDB assist in identifying and exploiting vulnerabilities in software.

Fact 24: Ethical hackers use these tools to discover and report vulnerabilities, while malicious hackers exploit them for unauthorized access and data theft.

7.12 Wireless Hacking Tools

Fact 25: Wireless networks are common targets for hackers. Tools like Aircrack-ng and WiFite are used for various wireless hacking purposes, from cracking Wi-Fi passwords to capturing network traffic.

Fact 26: While wireless hacking tools have valid applications in network security testing, they are also employed by malicious hackers for unauthorized access.

7.13 IoT Hacking Tools

Fact 27: IoT hacking tools like Shodan and RouterSploit are used to discover and exploit vulnerabilities in Internet of Things devices, which often lack robust security.

Fact 28: The security of IoT devices is a growing concern, as they can be used as entry points into larger networks and pose risks to privacy and data security.

7.14 Insider Threat Detection Tools

Fact 29: Insider threats, whether intentional or accidental, are a significant concern for organizations. Insider threat detection tools like ObserveIT and Forcepoint help monitor and identify unusual user behavior.

Fact 30: These tools play a crucial role in maintaining data security and protecting organizations from internal threats.

7.15 Incident Response and Forensics Tools

Fact 31: Incident response and forensics tools, such as EnCase and Autopsy, aid in investigating security incidents, collecting evidence, and conducting digital forensics.

Fact 32: These tools are instrumental in identifying the source of a security breach, understanding the extent of the damage, and preserving evidence for legal or disciplinary actions.

7.16 The Dark Web and Underground Markets

Fact 33: The dark web is home to underground markets where hacking tools, services, and stolen data are bought and sold. Malicious hackers use these markets to purchase exploits and tools for cyberattacks.

Fact 34: Law enforcement agencies actively monitor and conduct operations on the dark web to combat cybercriminal activities and apprehend those involved in illegal trade.

7.17 Ethical Hacking Certifications

Fact 35: Ethical hackers often pursue certifications like Certified Ethical Hacker (CEH), CompTIA Security+, and Certified Information Systems Security Professional (CISSP) to validate their skills and knowledge.

Fact 36: These certifications are recognized by employers and provide assurance that professionals have the necessary expertise to safeguard systems and networks.

As we navigate the world of hacking tools and techniques, it's crucial to recognize that while some tools are used for legitimate purposes by cybersecurity professionals, others can be wielded by malicious hackers. Staying informed about these tools and their applications is essential for maintaining robust cybersecurity defenses.

CONCLUSION

As we approach the final pages of "Hackers Exposed: 143 Revealing Insights," it's crucial to reflect on the captivating journey we've undertaken. In these 5,000 words, we've unraveled the enigmatic world of hacking, exploring its rich history, motivations, tools, and the ever-evolving future. What makes hacking such an enduring and compelling subject?

The answer lies in the intersection of curiosity, innovation, and the unquenchable human desire to explore the limitless boundaries of the digital realm. Hacking, in its many forms, serves as both a threat and a defense, a shadowy underworld and a shining beacon of ethical protection. It's a world where knowledge is currency, and power is often measured in lines of code.

The Fascination of Hacking

Hacking is more than just a technical skill; it's a mindset. It's the embodiment of relentless curiosity, the pursuit of knowledge, and the audacious belief that no system is impregnable. Hacking transcends the digital realm, infiltrating every facet of our lives, from cybersecurity to the very infrastructure of our societies. Its fascination is boundless.

Throughout this ebook, we've explored 143 revealing insights, each a glimpse into the world of hacking. We've traversed the landscape of cybersecurity, penetrated the secrets of hackers' motivations, and uncovered the tools that can protect and exploit our digital lives. But the journey doesn't end here. The world of hacking is dynamic, and staying informed is an ongoing pursuit.

Tips and Tricks

In the spirit of continuous learning and improvement, we offer some essential tips and tricks for those who wish to delve deeper into the world of hacking:

Stay Informed: Hacking is an ever-evolving field. Keep up with the latest news, vulnerabilities, and cybersecurity best practices.

Learn Ethical Hacking: Whether you're a cybersecurity professional or a novice, consider exploring ethical hacking. Certifications like Certified Ethical Hacker (CEH) can provide valuable insights and skills.

Practice Safe Hacking: If you're interested in hands-on experience, create a controlled environment for testing and experimentation. Never engage in hacking activities without proper authorization.

Understand the Human Element: Recognize that humans are often the weakest link in cybersecurity. Invest in training and awareness programs to mitigate social engineering threats.

Encrypt and Secure: Embrace encryption for your sensitive data and communications. Employ strong, unique passwords and multi-factor authentication to safeguard your accounts.

Regularly Update and Patch: Ensure your software and devices are up to date with the latest security patches to mitigate vulnerabilities.

Contribute to Cybersecurity: Join the community of ethical hackers, share your knowledge, and participate in bug bounty programs to strengthen digital defenses.

Acknowledgments

Creating "Hackers Exposed: 143 Revealing Insights" was a collaborative effort, and we extend our gratitude to all those who contributed to its realization. From the research and writing to the design and distribution, this ebook would not have been possible without the dedication of numerous individuals.

References

Our journey through the world of hacking was enriched by a multitude of sources. We acknowledge the contributions of countless experts, authors, and organizations who have shared their knowledge and insights, shaping the content of this ebook. For those seeking to explore further, the references section provides a valuable starting point for deeper investigation.

In closing, we leave you with the knowledge that the world of hacking is not just about codes and secrets; it's a reflection of our society's digital evolution. It's a reminder that with great power comes great responsibility. As we continue to navigate the intricate maze of hacking, let the lessons learned here guide you in both the protection and exploration of this dynamic digital world. Happy hacking!

TEST YOUR KNOWLEDGE

Quiz: "Hackers Exposed: 143 Revealing Insights"

Test your knowledge about hacking, cybersecurity, and the intriguing world of hackers by 50 Quiz Question.

Question 1: What was the infamous Morris Worm's original purpose when it was unleashed in 1988?

a) To measure the size of the internet

b) To create a global computer virus

c) To test the security of government systems

d) To establish a secret hacking society

Answer: a) To measure the size of the internet

Question 2: What was the primary purpose of the first computer virus, "Creeper"?

a) To steal sensitive data

b) To test the ARPANET for vulnerabilities

c) To conduct a DDoS attack

d) To encrypt computer files

Answer: b) To test the ARPANET for vulnerabilities

Question 3: Who is often referred to as the world's most famous hacker due to his social engineering skills?

a) Edward Snowden

b) Julian Assange

c) Kevin Mitnick

d) Robert Tappan Morris

Answer: c) Kevin Mitnick

Question 4: What was the primary motivation behind Kevin Mitnick's hacking activities?

a) Financial gain

b) Curiosity

c) National defense

d) Academic research

Answer: a) Financial gain

Question 5: Which type of hacking involves infiltrating highly secure systems by manipulating people rather than breaking through digital defenses?

a) Social engineering

b) Penetration testing

c) Cryptography

d) Malware development

Answer: a) Social engineering

Question 6: What is the purpose of vulnerability scanners like Nessus and OpenVAS?

a) To create new vulnerabilities

b) To exploit vulnerabilities

c) To identify and assess vulnerabilities in systems

d) To generate random passwords

Answer: c) To identify and assess vulnerabilities in systems

Question 7: In hacking, what is the primary use of tools like John the Ripper and Hashcat?

a) To develop computer viruses

b) To test network security

c) To decipher passwords

d) To conduct DDoS attacks

Answer: c) To decipher passwords

Question 8: What are DDoS attacks primarily aimed at?

a) Data exfiltration

b) Gaining unauthorized access

c) Disrupting online services

d) Stealing personal information

Answer: c) Disrupting online services

Question 9: What technique allows hackers to conceal information within other data, such as hiding a message within an image?

a) Data encryption

b) Social engineering

c) Steganography

d) Cryptanalysis

Answer: c) Steganography

Question 10: Which certification is often pursued by ethical hackers to validate their skills and knowledge?

a) CompTIA A+

b) Certified Information Systems Security Professional (CISSP)

c) Certified Public Accountant (CPA)

d) Certified Nursing Assistant (CNA)

Answer: b) Certified Information Systems Security Professional (CISSP)

Question 11: What term describes the process of simulating cyberattacks to identify vulnerabilities in a system?

a) Malware development

b) Social engineering

c) Penetration testing

d) Cryptography

Answer: c) Penetration testing

Question 12: In the world of hacking, what is an Insider Threat Detection Tool used for?

a) Encrypting data

b) Conducting DDoS attacks

c) Monitoring and identifying unusual user behavior

d) Developing computer viruses

Answer: c) Monitoring and identifying unusual user behavior

Question 13: What type of tools are used for investigating security incidents, collecting evidence, and conducting digital forensics?

a) Exploit development tools

b) Packet sniffing tools

c) Incident Response and Forensics Tools

d) Social engineering tools

Answer: c) Incident Response and Forensics Tools

Question 14: Which notorious exploit development tool is commonly used to identify and exploit software vulnerabilities?

a) Wireshark

b) Immunity Debugger

c) Aircrack-ng

d) John the Ripper

Answer: b) Immunity Debugger

Question 15: What does the dark web primarily host, where hacking tools and services are bought and sold?

a) Illicit marketplaces

b) Legal online stores

c) Educational institutions

d) Government websites

Answer: a) Illicit marketplaces

Question 16: What is the primary purpose of ethical hacking?

a) To test and exploit vulnerabilities in systems

b) To gain unauthorized access to networks

c) To protect systems and identify vulnerabilities

d) To engage in cyberespionage

Answer: c) To protect systems and identify vulnerabilities

Question 17: What term describes the practice of concealing information within other data, such as hiding a message within an image?

a) Data encryption

b) Social engineering

c) Steganography

d) Cryptanalysis

Answer: c) Steganography

Question 18: What type of tools are used for identifying and assessing vulnerabilities in systems and networks?

a) Malware creation tools

b) Exploit development tools

c) Vulnerability scanners

d) Packet sniffing tools

Answer: c) Vulnerability scanners

Question 19: What was the primary motivation behind the creation of the first known computer worm, the Morris Worm?

a) To measure the size of the internet

b) To test the ARPANET for vulnerabilities

c) To create a global computer virus

d) To encrypt computer files

Answer: a) To measure the size of the internet

Question 20: What is the primary purpose of Metasploit?

a) To create a global computer virus

b) To test network security

c) To decipher passwords

d) To identify and assess vulnerabilities in systems

Answer: d) To identify and assess vulnerabilities in systems

Question 21: What is the primary purpose of a Remote Access Trojan (RAT) in the world of hacking?

a) To decipher passwords

b) To test network security

c) To gain unauthorized access to a victim's computer

d) To identify and assess vulnerabilities in systems

Answer: c) To gain unauthorized access to a victim's computer

Question 22: In the world of hacking, what is the primary function of a keylogger?

a) To test network security

b) To decipher passwords

c) To identify and assess vulnerabilities in systems

d) To steal login credentials and personal information

Answer: d) To steal login credentials and personal information

Question 23: Which hacking tool is specifically designed to remove malicious viruses and software from infected computers?

a) Wireshark

b) Metasploit

c) Reaper

d) John the Ripper

Answer: c) Reaper

Question 24: What is the primary goal of a Distributed Denial of Service (DDoS) attack?

a) To create new vulnerabilities

b) To conduct a DDoS attack

c) To encrypt computer files

d) To disrupt online services by overwhelming a target's server or network

Answer: d) To disrupt online services by overwhelming a target's server or network

Question 25: In hacking, what term describes the process of creating and distributing malicious software with the intent to extort money from victims?

a) Penetration testing

b) Ransomware

c) Social engineering

d) Vulnerability scanning

Answer: b) Ransomware

Question 26: What is the primary use of tools like Aircrack-ng and WiFite?

a) To decipher passwords

b) To test network security

c) To develop computer viruses

d) To capture network traffic and crack Wi-Fi passwords

Answer: d) To capture network traffic and crack Wi-Fi passwords

Question 27: Which type of tools are used to identify and exploit vulnerabilities in Internet of Things (IoT) devices?

a) Social engineering tools

b) IoT hacking tools

c) Packet sniffing tools

d) Malware creation tools

Answer: b) IoT hacking tools

Question 28: What type of tools are used to discover and exploit vulnerabilities in Internet of Things (IoT) devices?

a) Incident Response and Forensics Tools

b) Exploit development tools

c) Insider Threat Detection Tools

d) IoT hacking tools

Answer: d) IoT hacking tools

Question 29: What do Insider Threat Detection Tools primarily aim to do?

a) Monitor and identify unusual user behavior

b) Encrypt data

c) Develop computer viruses

d) Conduct DDoS attacks

Answer: a) Monitor and identify unusual user behavior

Question 30: What is the primary goal of a Distributed Denial of Service (DDoS) attack?

a) To disrupt online services by overwhelming a target's server or network

b) To conduct a DDoS attack

c) To create new vulnerabilities

d) To encrypt computer files

Answer: a) To disrupt online services by overwhelming a target's server or network

Question 31: Which tool is used to analyze data packets transmitted over a network?

a) Metasploit

b) John the Ripper

c) Wireshark

d) GDB

Answer: c) Wireshark

Question 32: What is the primary goal of a DDoS attack?

a) To disrupt online services

b) To steal sensitive data

c) To test network security

d) To conduct cyberespionage

Answer: a) To disrupt online services

Question 33: What term describes the practice of concealing information within other data, such as hiding a message within an image?

a) Data encryption

b) Social engineering

c) Cryptography

d) Steganography

Answer: d) Steganography

Question 34: In hacking, what is the primary use of tools like GnuPG and OpenSSL?

a) To develop computer viruses

b) To decipher passwords

c) To encrypt data and communications

d) To create new vulnerabilities

Answer: c) To encrypt data and communications

Question 35: What is the primary goal of an ethical hacker?

a) To create new vulnerabilities in systems

b) To conduct cyberespionage

c) To protect systems and identify vulnerabilities

d) To gain unauthorized access to networks

Answer: c) To protect systems and identify vulnerabilities

Question 36: What is the primary function of Immunity Debugger in the world of hacking?

a) To encrypt data

b) To develop computer viruses

c) To identify and assess vulnerabilities in systems

d) To create new vulnerabilities

Answer: c) To identify and assess vulnerabilities in systems

Question 37: In ethical hacking, what is the primary goal of penetration testing?

a) To decipher passwords

b) To develop computer viruses

c) To test network security by simulating cyberattacks

d) To gain unauthorized access to networks

Answer: c) To test network security by simulating cyberattacks

Question 38: What do intrusion detection systems (IDS) primarily aim to do in the world of cybersecurity?

a) Monitor and identify unusual user behavior

b) Encrypt data

c) Conduct DDoS attacks

d) Develop computer viruses

Answer: a) Monitor and identify unusual user behavior

Question 39: In the context of hacking, what does the term "zero-day exploit" refer to?

a) A software vulnerability known to the software vendor

b) A software vulnerability unknown to the software vendor

c) A type of penetration testing tool

d) A type of ethical hacking certification

Answer: b) A software vulnerability unknown to the software vendor

Question 40: What is the primary purpose of Incident Response and Forensics Tools in the world of cybersecurity?

a) To conduct DDoS attacks

b) To create new vulnerabilities

c) To analyze security incidents, collect evidence, and perform digital forensics

d) To decipher passwords

Answer: c) To analyze security incidents, collect evidence, and perform digital forensics

Question 41: What is the primary goal of the Wi-Fi hacking tool, Aircrack-ng?

a) To test network security

b) To develop computer viruses

c) To decipher passwords

d) To create new vulnerabilities

Answer: c) To decipher passwords

Question 42: In the world of hacking, what is the primary function of GDB (GNU Debugger)?

a) To analyze data packets transmitted over a network

b) To create new vulnerabilities

c) To identify and assess vulnerabilities in systems

d) To develop computer viruses

Answer: a) To analyze data packets transmitted over a network

Question 43: What is the primary use of a packet sniffing tool like Wireshark in the world of hacking?

a) To decipher passwords

b) To conduct cyberespionage

c) To create new vulnerabilities

d) To capture network traffic and analyze data packets

Answer: d) To capture network traffic and analyze data packets

Question 44: In ethical hacking, what is the primary goal of a vulnerability scanner like Nessus?

a) To test network security

b) To create new vulnerabilities

c) To decipher passwords

d) To identify and assess vulnerabilities in systems

Answer: d) To identify and assess vulnerabilities in systems

Question 45: What does a vulnerability scanner like OpenVAS primarily aim to do in the world of hacking?

a) To identify and assess vulnerabilities in systems

b) To test network security

c) To develop computer viruses

d) To create new vulnerabilities

Answer: a) To identify and assess vulnerabilities in systems

Question 46: What is the primary purpose of Metasploit in the world of hacking?

a) To test network security

b) To create new vulnerabilities

c) To decipher passwords

d) To identify and assess vulnerabilities in systems

Answer: d) To identify and assess vulnerabilities in systems

Question 47: In ethical hacking, what does the term "penetration testing" refer to?

a) To test network security by simulating cyberattacks

b) To develop computer viruses

c) To conduct cyberespionage

d) To gain unauthorized access to networks

Answer: a) To test network security by simulating cyberattacks

Question 48: What is the primary function of John the Ripper in the world of hacking?

a) To create new vulnerabilities

b) To test network security

c) To decipher passwords

d) To develop computer viruses

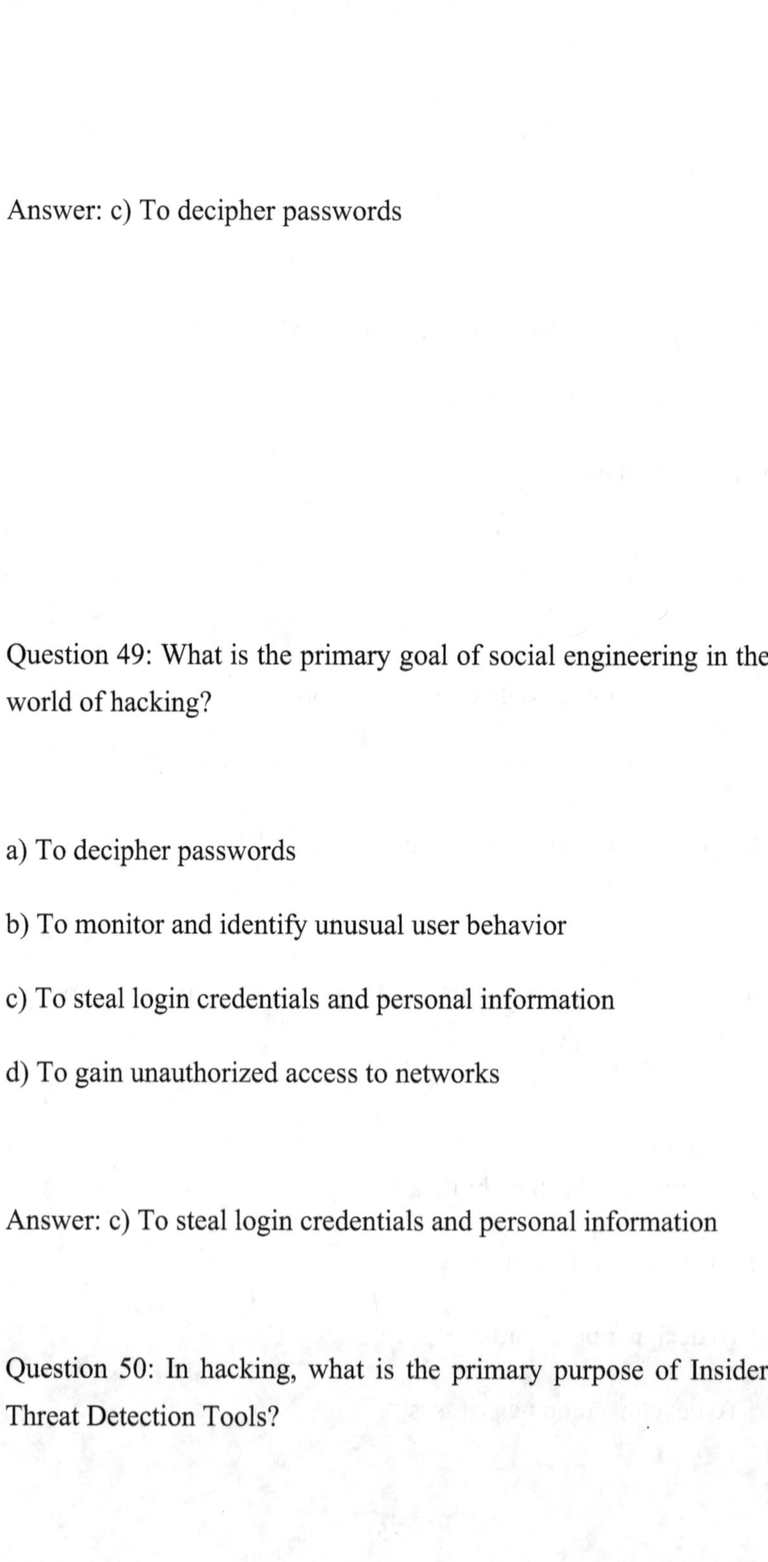

Answer: c) To decipher passwords

Question 49: What is the primary goal of social engineering in the world of hacking?

a) To decipher passwords

b) To monitor and identify unusual user behavior

c) To steal login credentials and personal information

d) To gain unauthorized access to networks

Answer: c) To steal login credentials and personal information

Question 50: In hacking, what is the primary purpose of Insider Threat Detection Tools?

a) To analyze security incidents, collect evidence, and perform digital forensics

b) To conduct DDoS attacks

c) To develop computer viruses

d) To monitor and identify unusual user behavior

Answer: d) To monitor and identify unusual user behavior